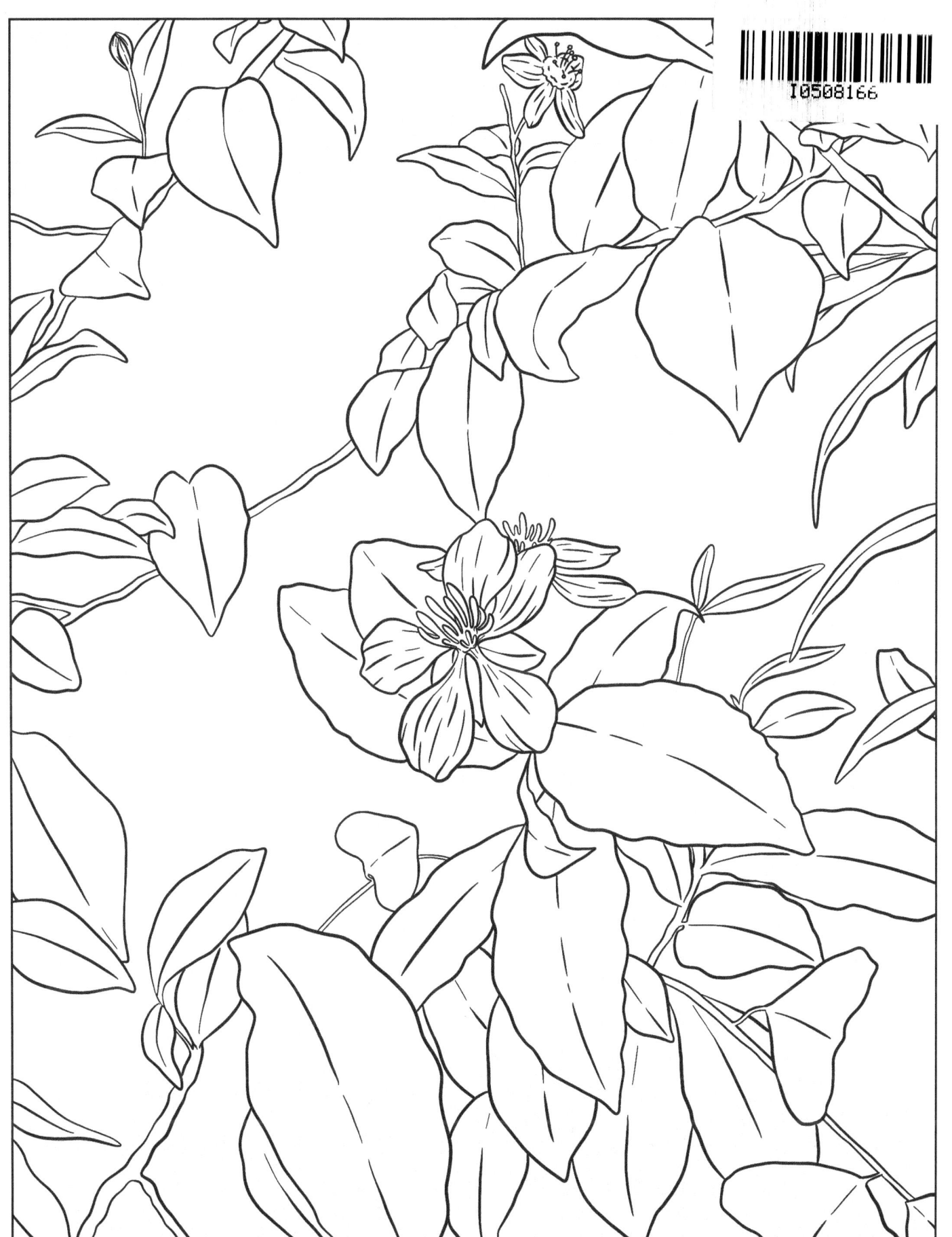

SCRIBBLE PAGE!

We've left this page blank, so you can test out your colors, cut out and frame your artwork, practice drawing flowers yourself, or tear it out and trace the designs onto watercolor paper, and have a go at painting them instead!

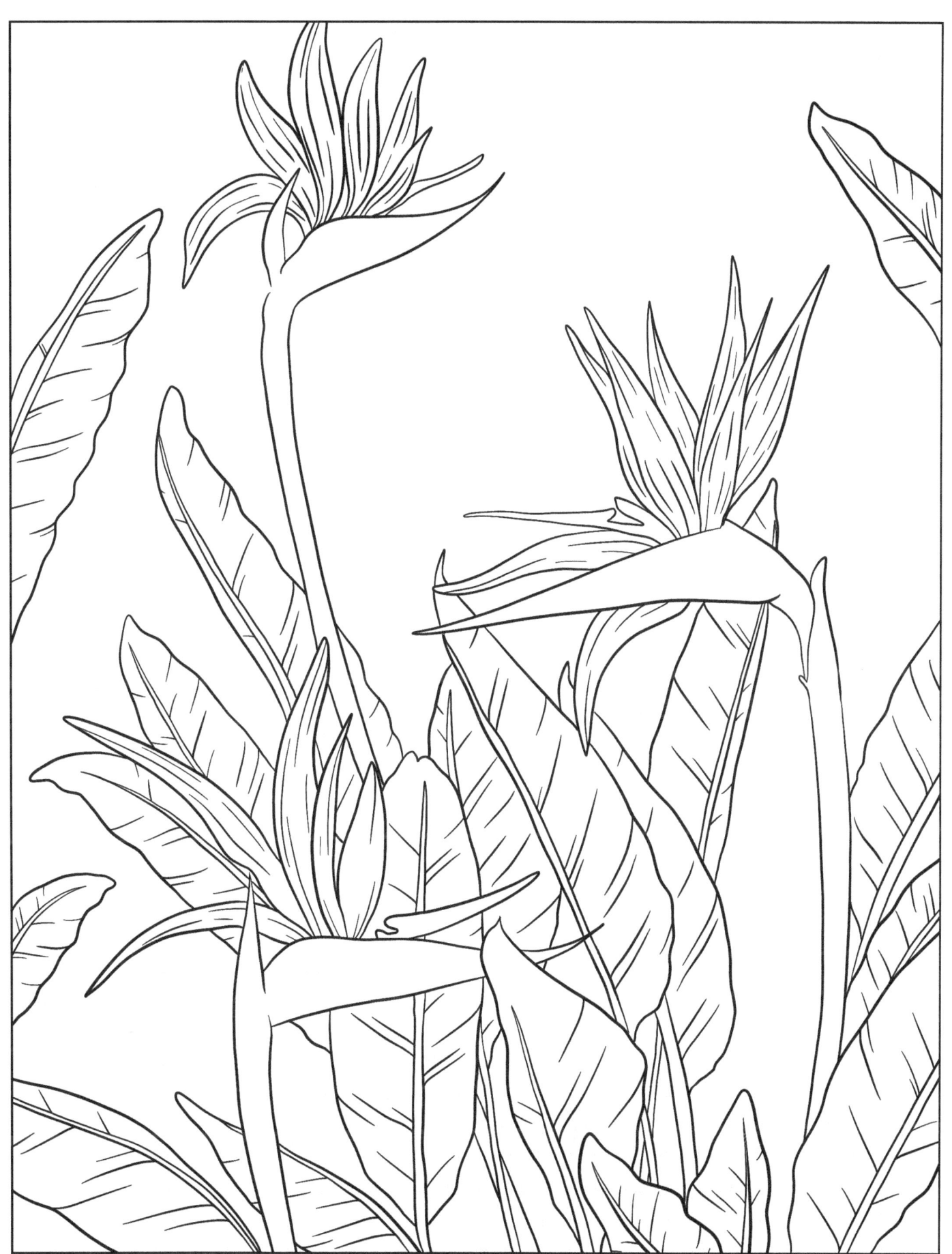

SCRIBBLE PAGE!

We've left this page blank, so you can test out your colors, cut out and frame your artwork, practice drawing flowers yourself, or tear it out and trace the designs onto watercolor paper, and have a go at painting them instead!

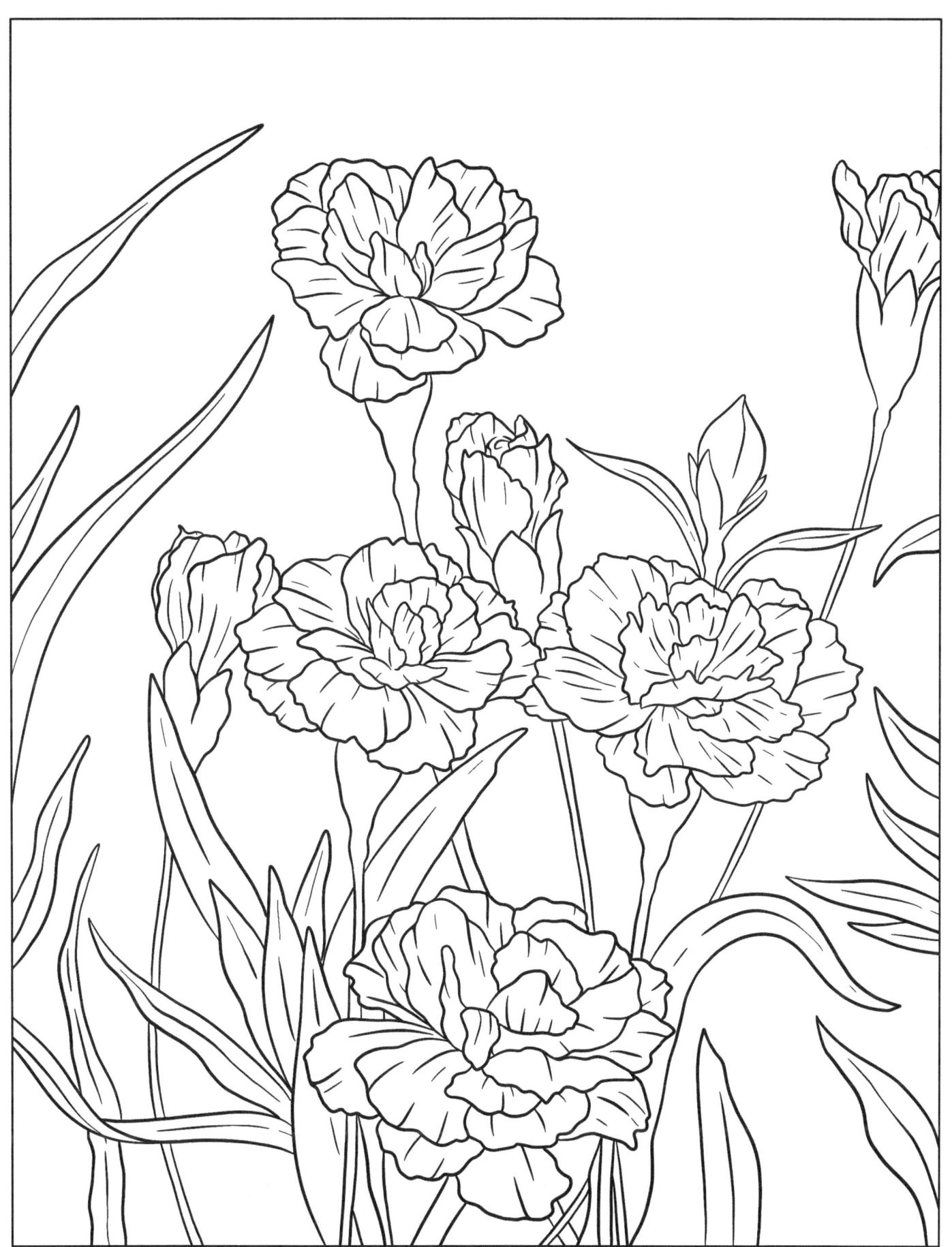

SCRIBBLE PAGE!

We've left this page blank, so you can test out your colors, cut out and frame your artwork, practice drawing flowers yourself, or tear it out and trace the designs onto watercolor paper, and have a go at painting them instead!

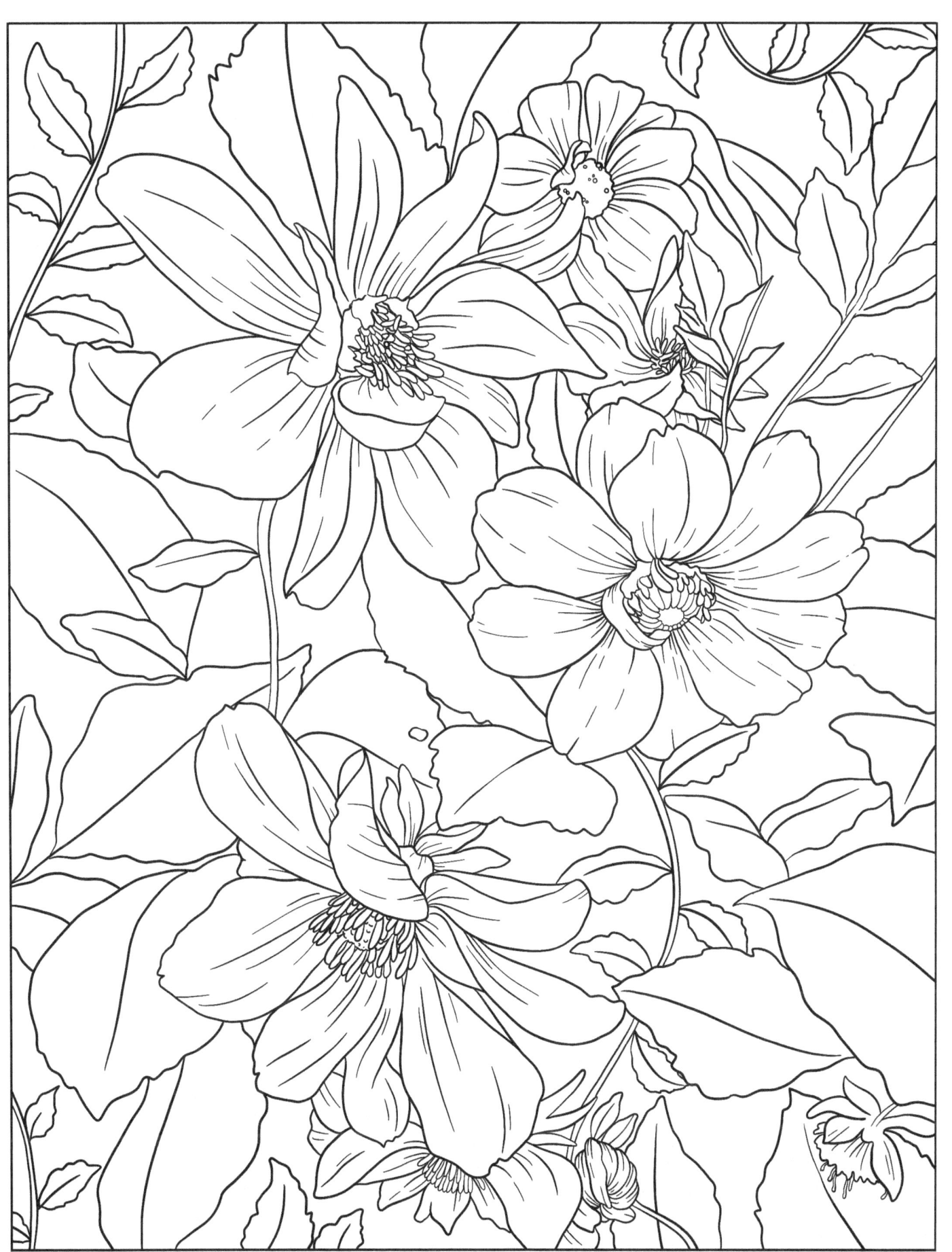

SCRIBBLE PAGE!

We've left this page blank, so you can test out your colors, cut out and frame your artwork, practice drawing flowers yourself, or tear it out and trace the designs onto watercolor paper, and have a go at painting them instead!

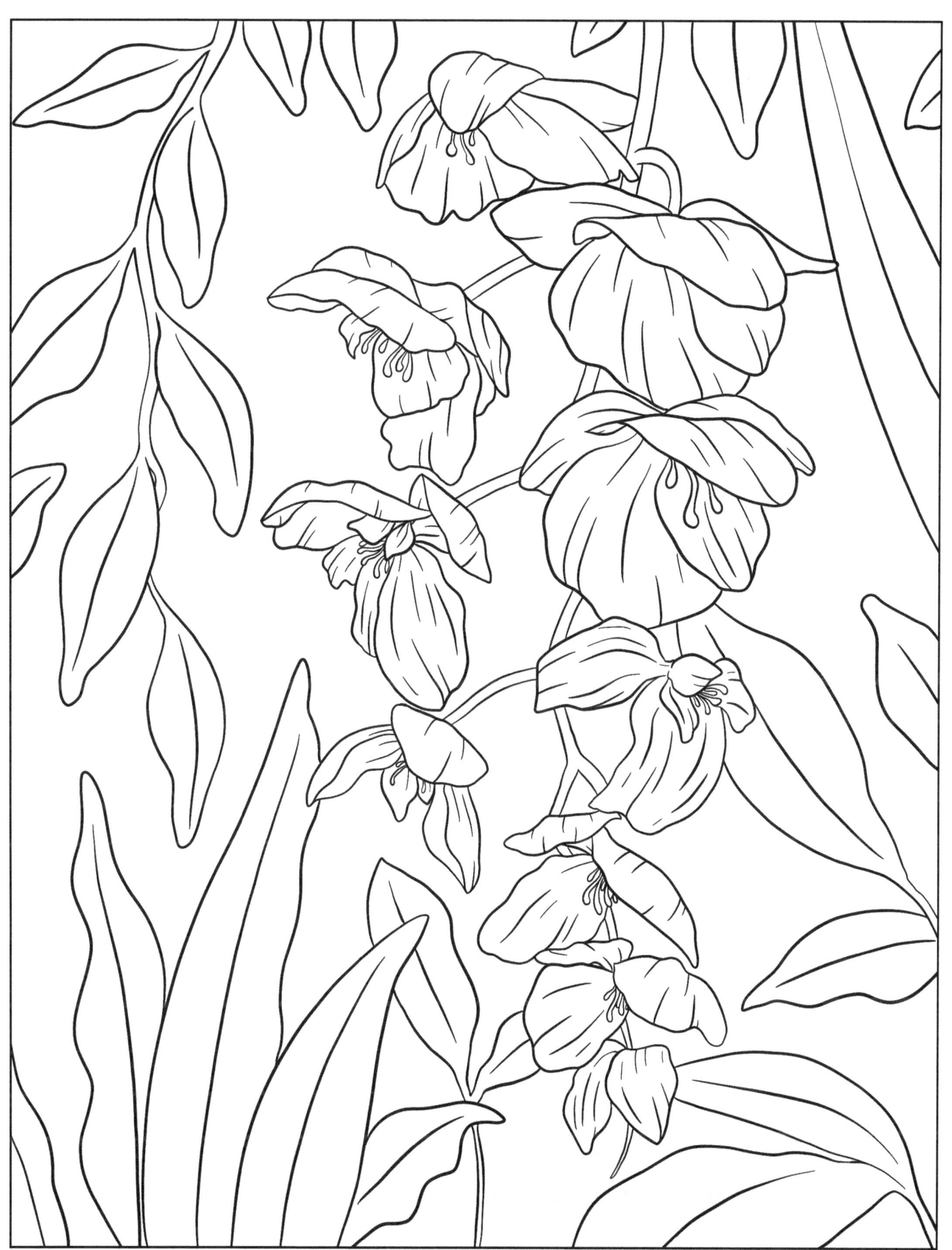

SCRIBBLE PAGE!

We've left this page blank, so you can test out your colors, cut out and frame your artwork, practice drawing flowers yourself, or tear it out and trace the designs onto watercolor paper, and have a go at painting them instead!

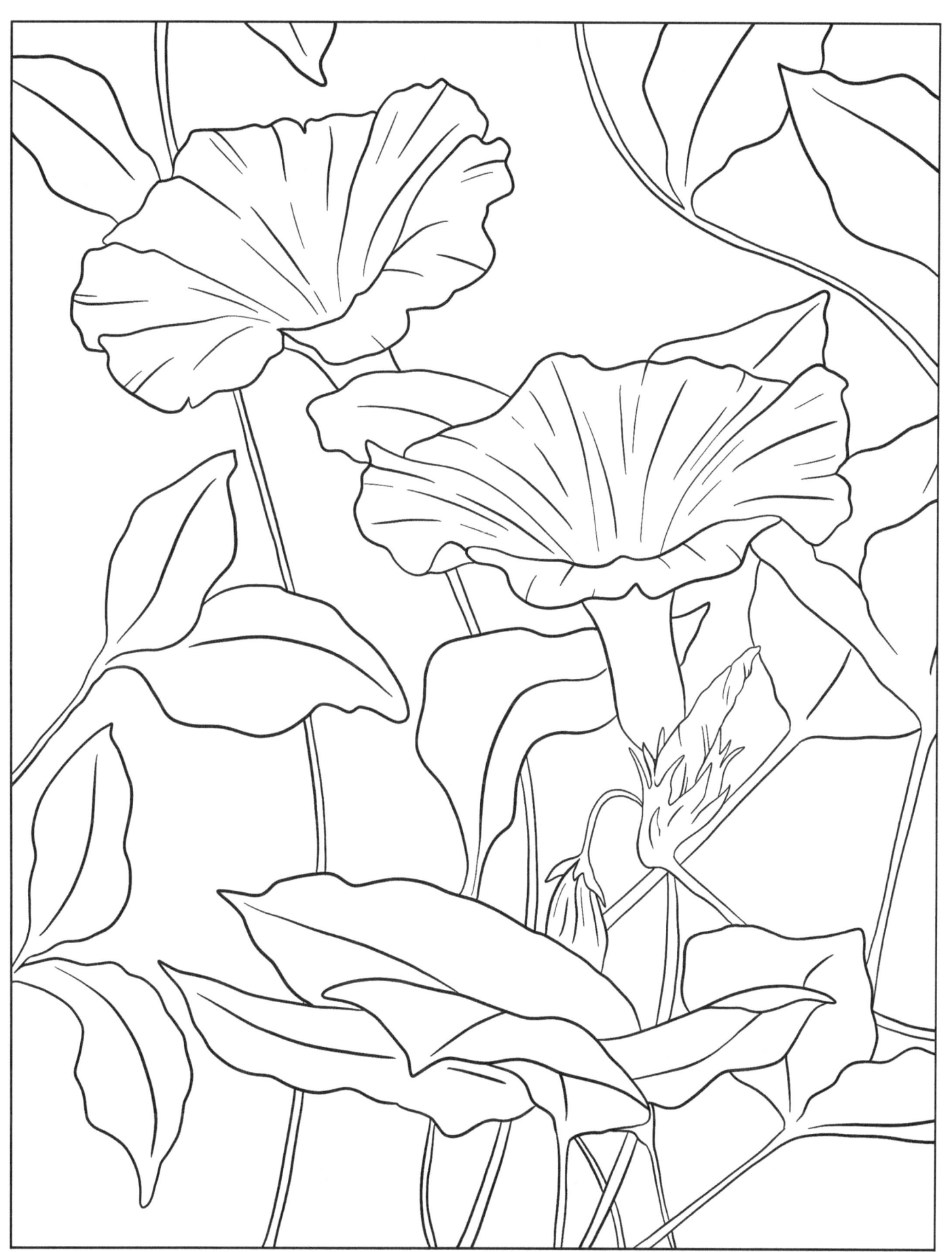

SCRIBBLE PAGE!

We've left this page blank, so you can test out your colors, cut out and frame your artwork, practice drawing flowers yourself, or tear it out and trace the designs onto watercolor paper, and have a go at painting them instead!

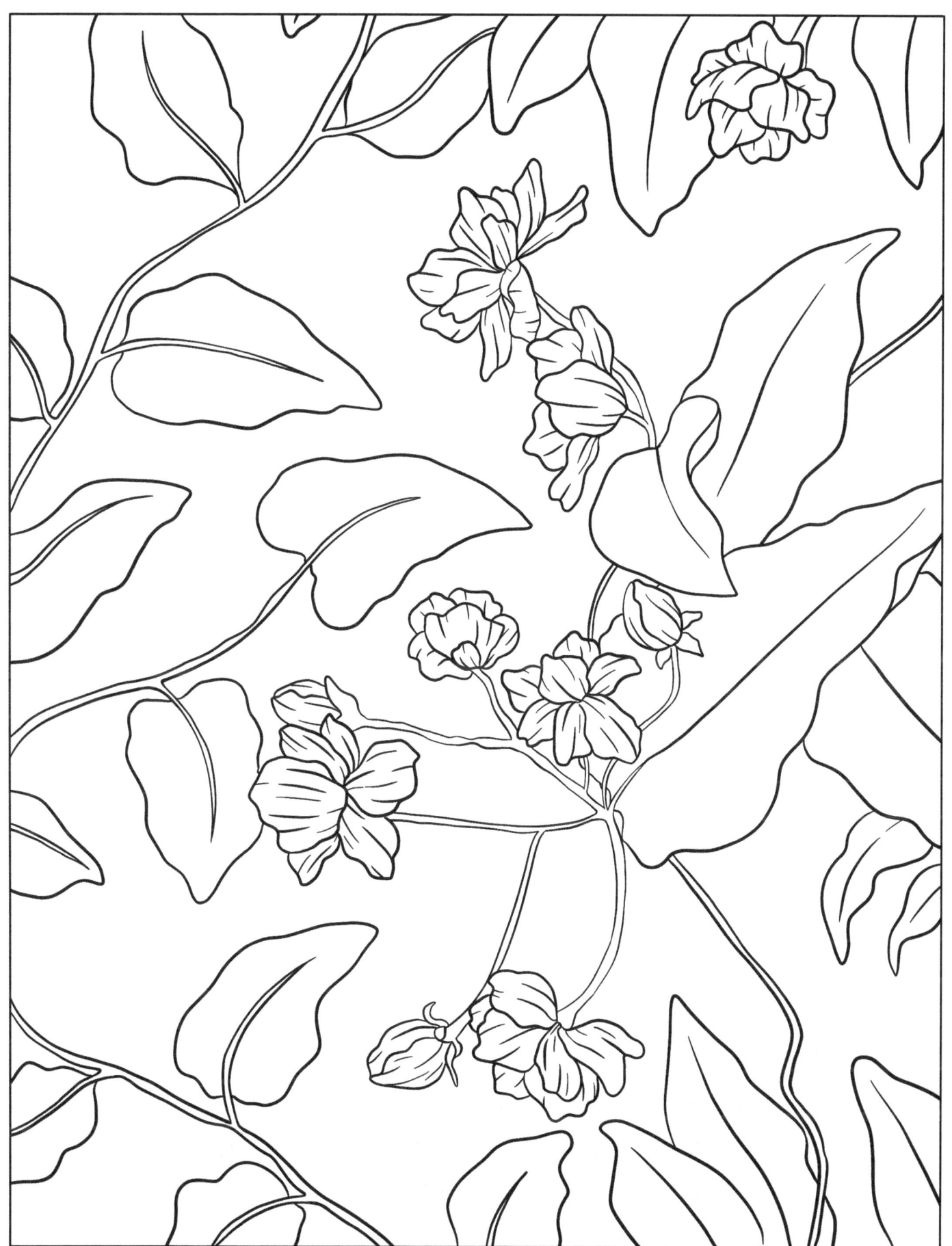

SCRIBBLE PAGE!

We've left this page blank, so you can test out your colors, cut out and frame your artwork, practice drawing flowers yourself, or tear it out and trace the designs onto watercolor paper, and have a go at painting them instead!

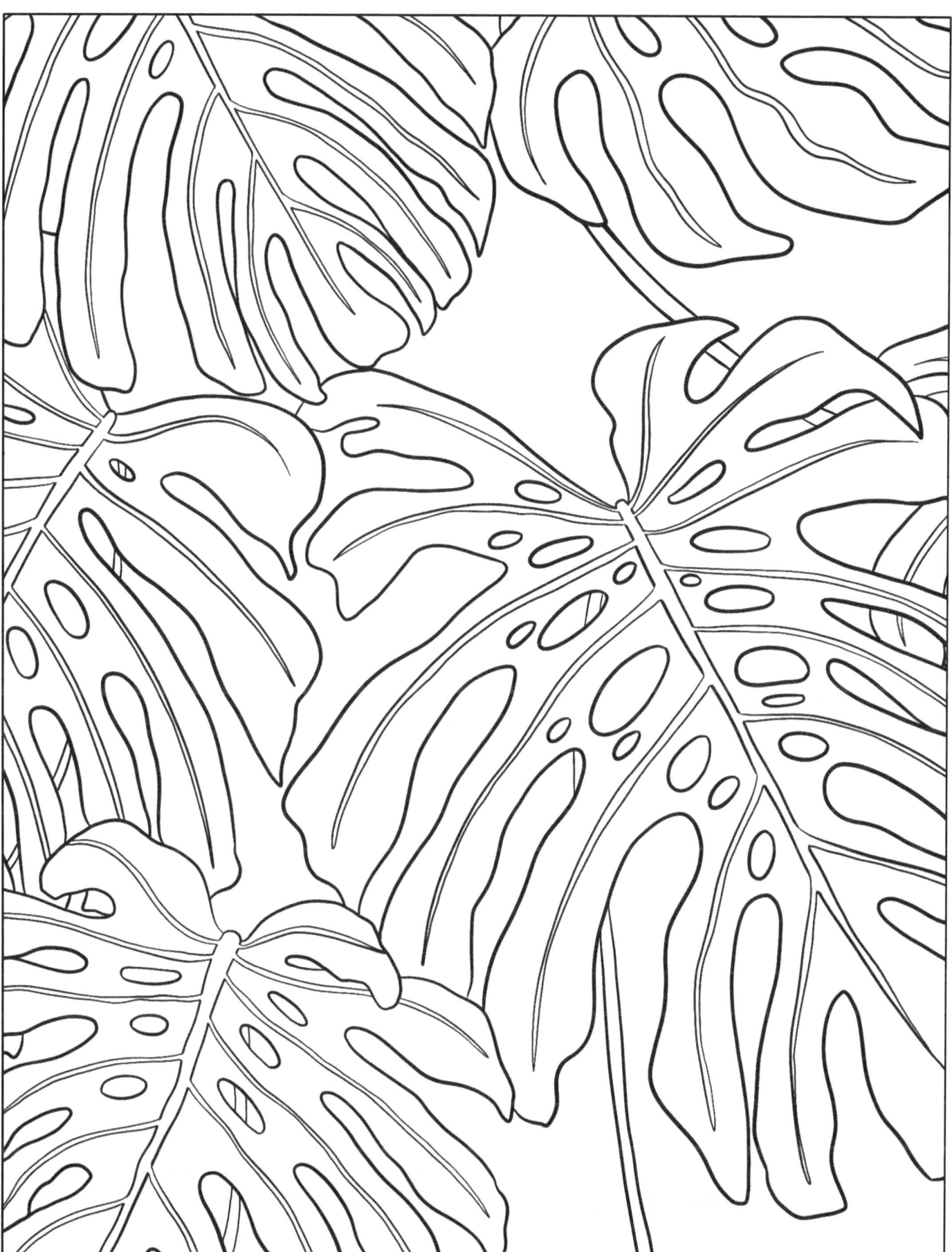

SCRIBBLE PAGE!

We've left this page blank, so you can test out your colors, cut out and frame your artwork, practice drawing flowers yourself, or tear it out and trace the designs onto watercolor paper, and have a go at painting them instead!

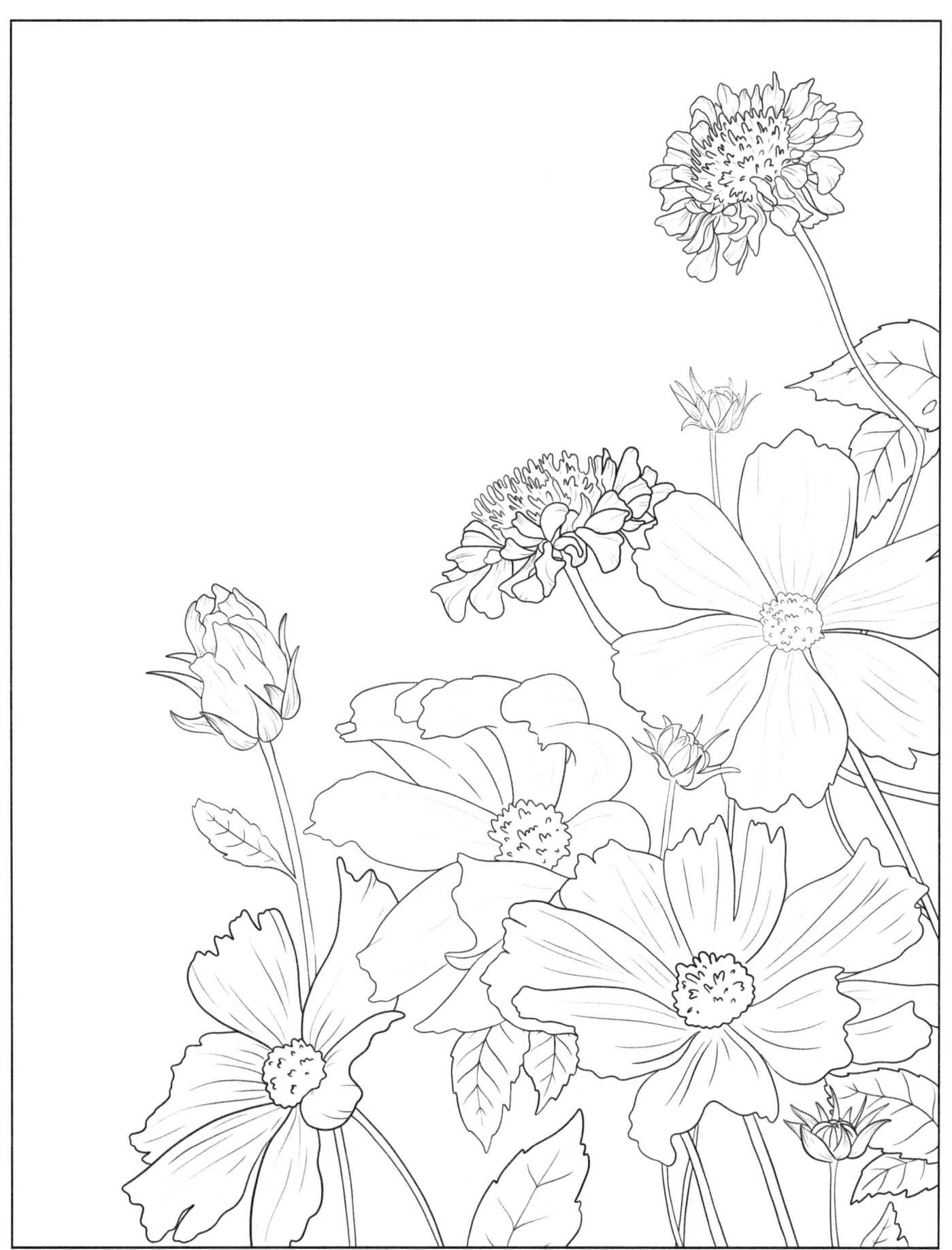

SCRIBBLE PAGE!

We've left this page blank, so you can test out your colors, cut out and frame your artwork, practice drawing flowers yourself, or tear it out and trace the designs onto watercolor paper, and have a go at painting them instead!

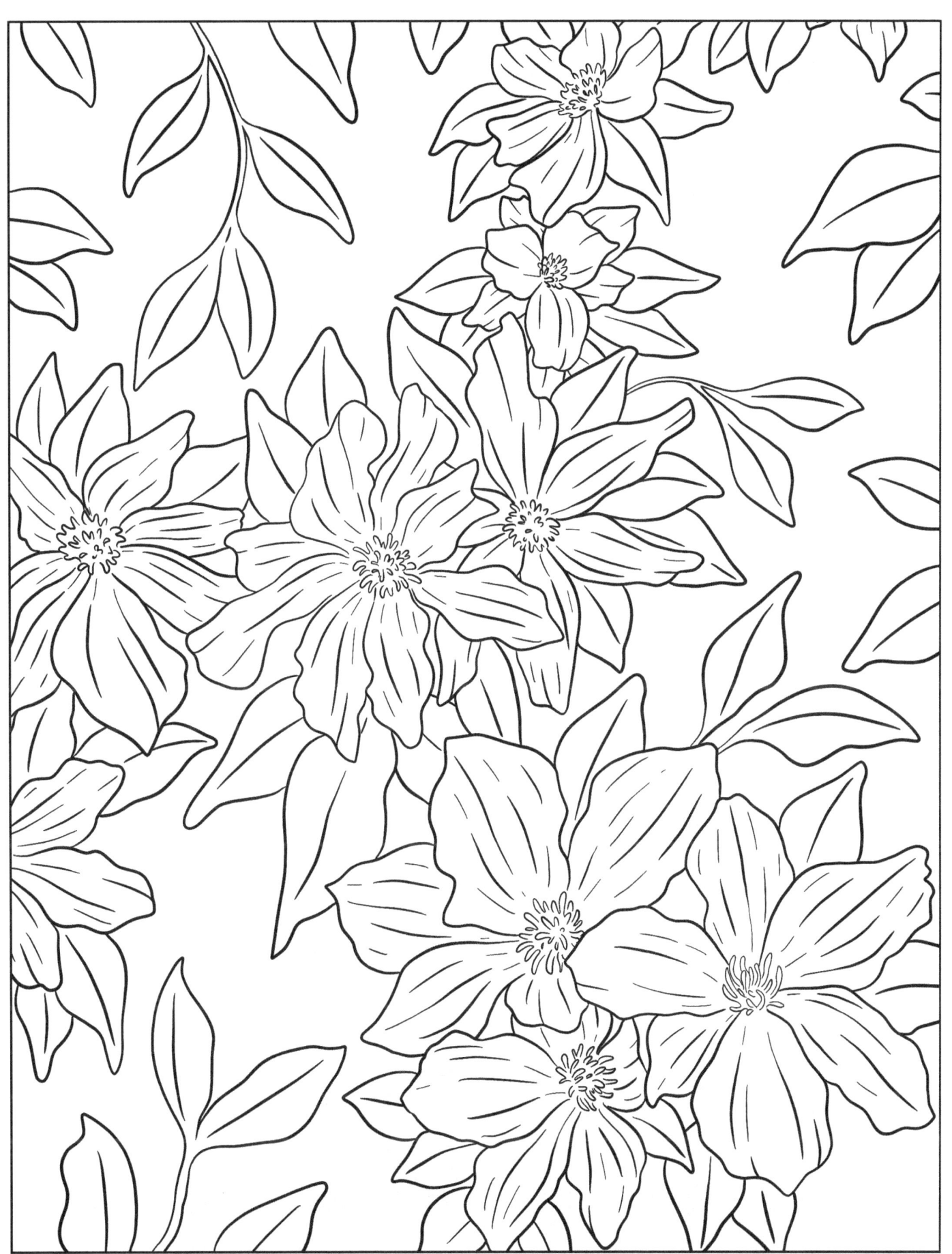

SCRIBBLE PAGE!

We've left this page blank, so you can test out your colors, cut out and frame your artwork, practice drawing flowers yourself, or tear it out and trace the designs onto watercolor paper, and have a go at painting them instead!

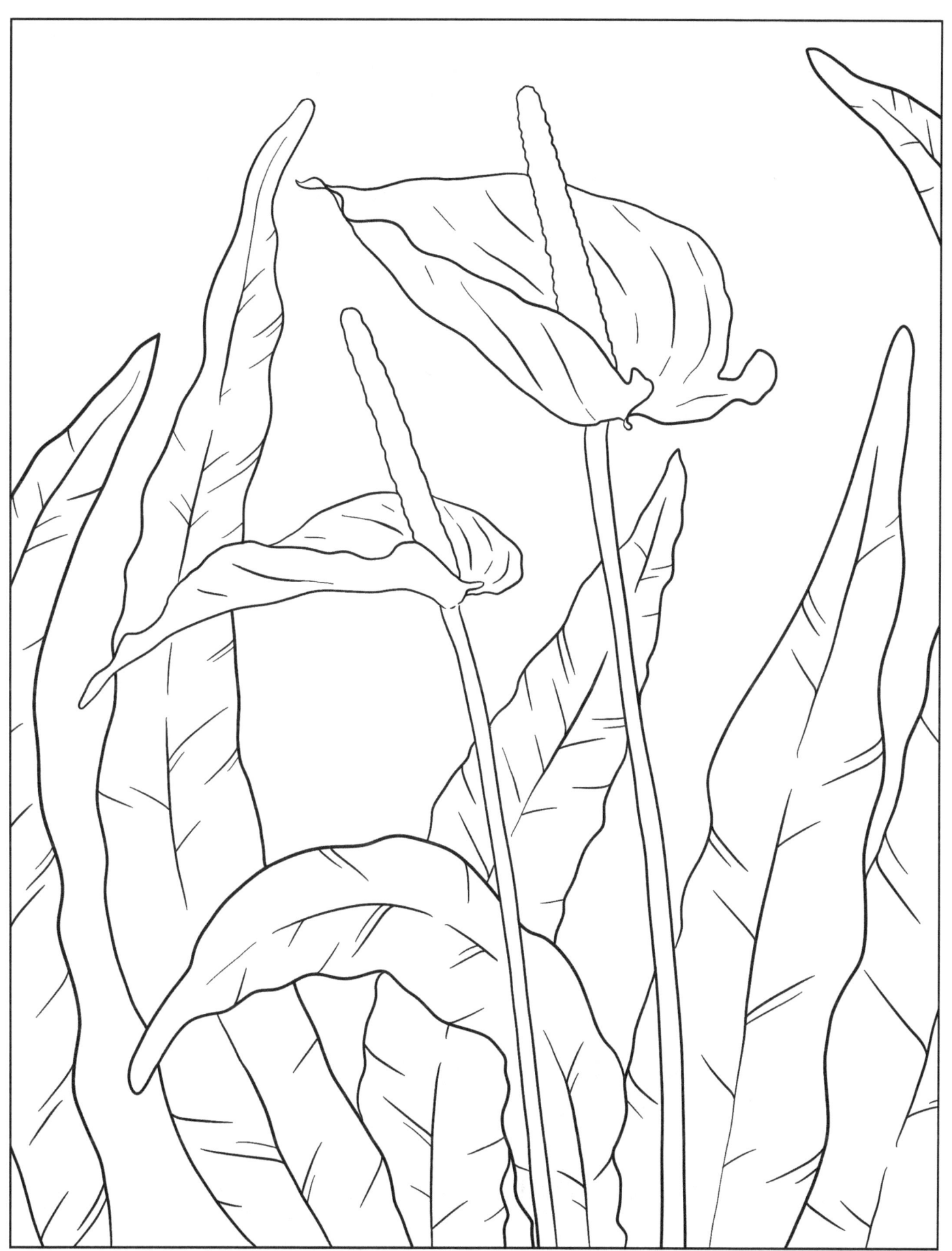

SCRIBBLE PAGE!

We've left this page blank, so you can test out your colors, cut out and frame your artwork, practice drawing flowers yourself, or tear it out and trace the designs onto watercolor paper, and have a go at painting them instead!

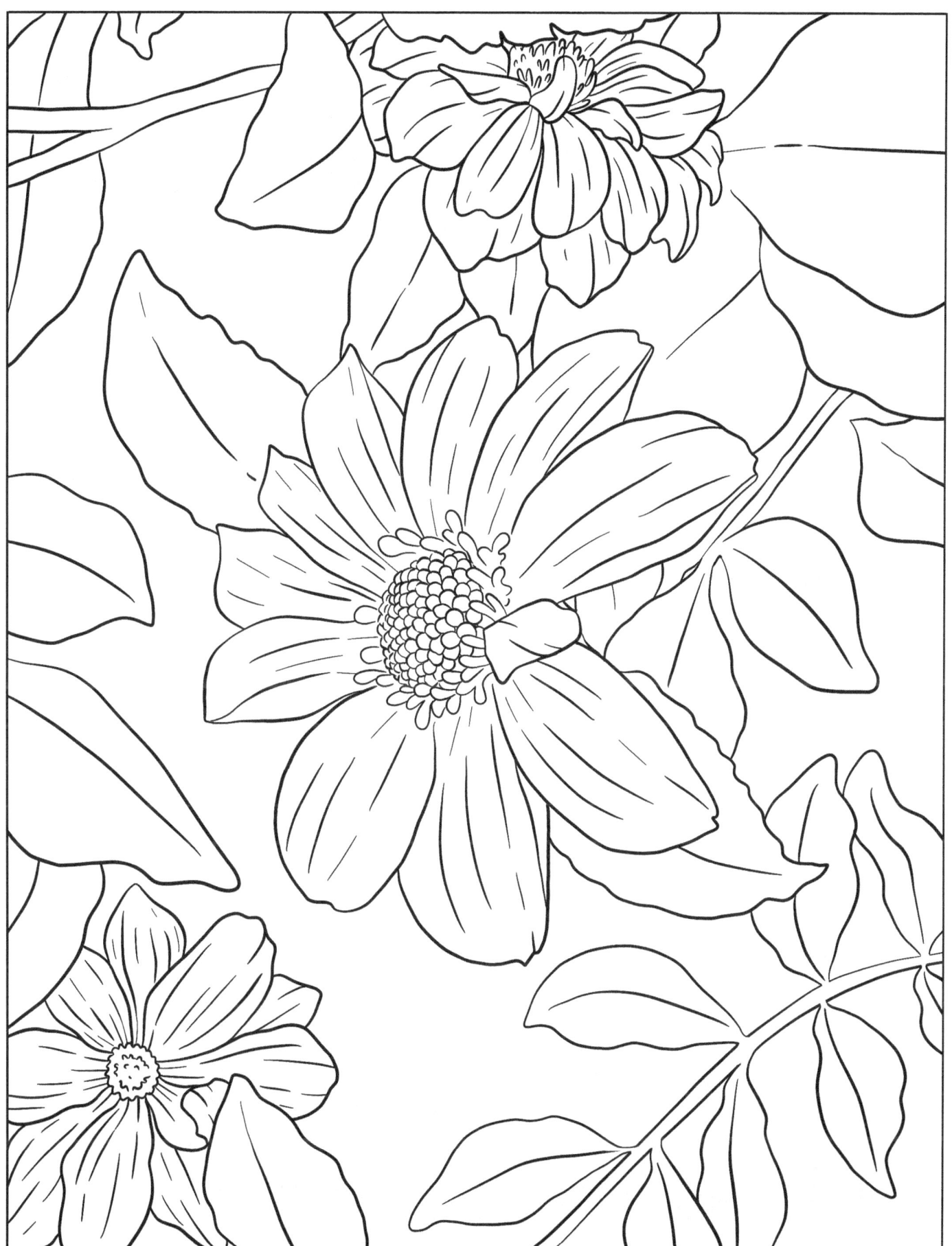

SCRIBBLE PAGE!

We've left this page blank, so you can test out your colors, cut out and frame your artwork, practice drawing flowers yourself, or tear it out and trace the designs onto watercolor paper, and have a go at painting them instead!

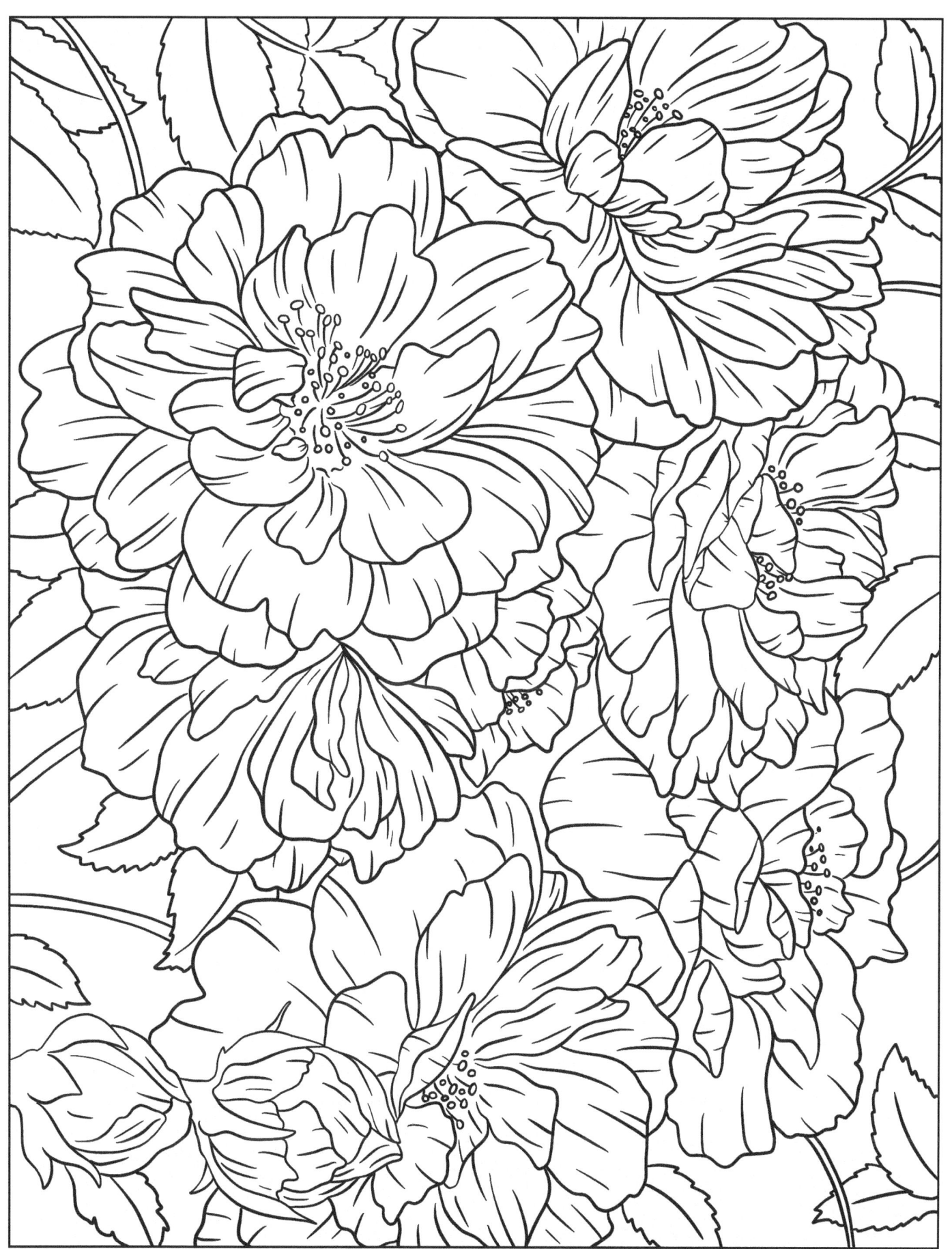

SCRIBBLE PAGE!

We've left this page blank, so you can test out your colors, cut out and frame your artwork, practice drawing flowers yourself, or tear it out and trace the designs onto watercolor paper, and have a go at painting them instead!

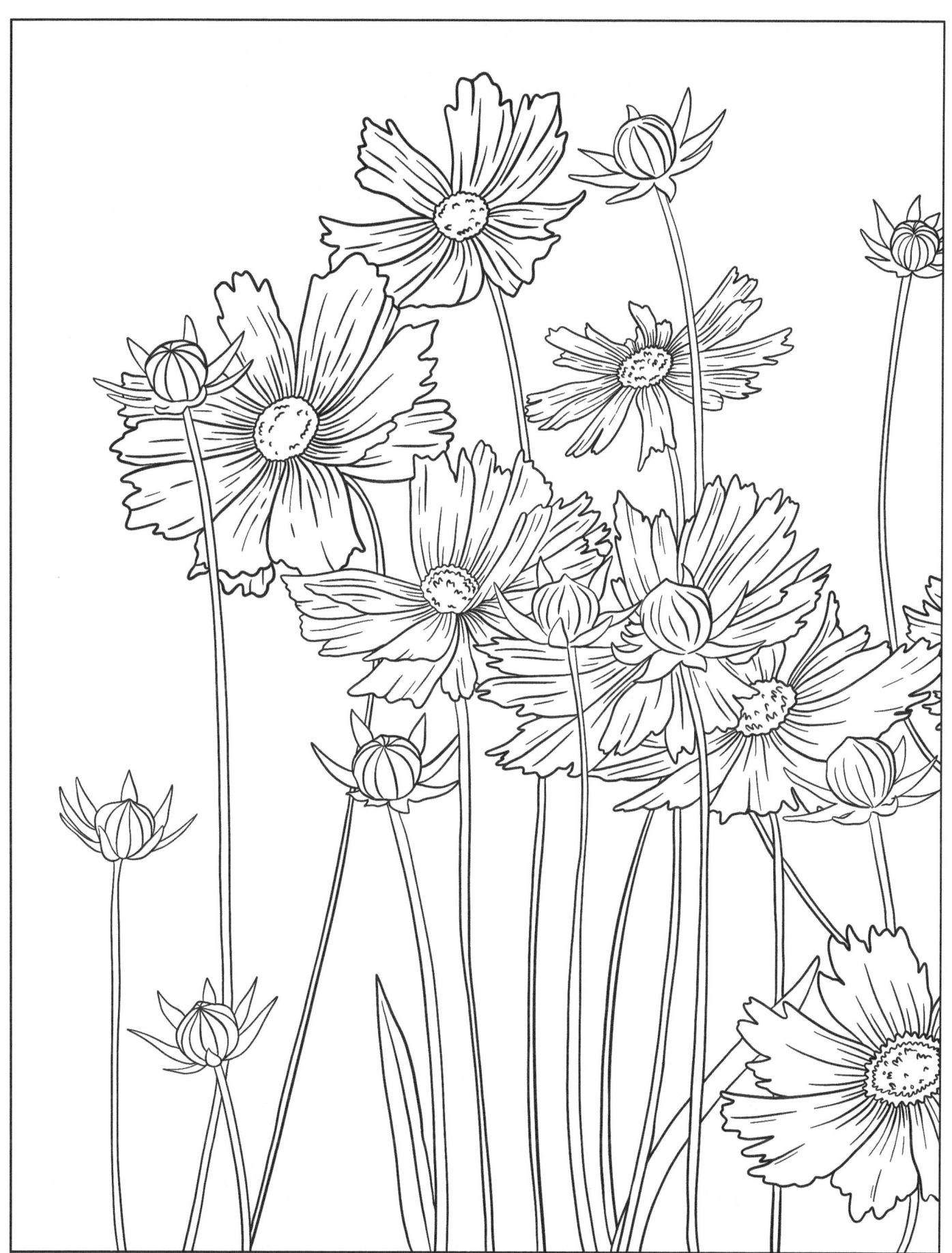

SCRIBBLE PAGE!

We've left this page blank, so you can test out your colors, cut out and frame your artwork, practice drawing flowers yourself, or tear it out and trace the designs onto watercolor paper, and have a go at painting them instead!

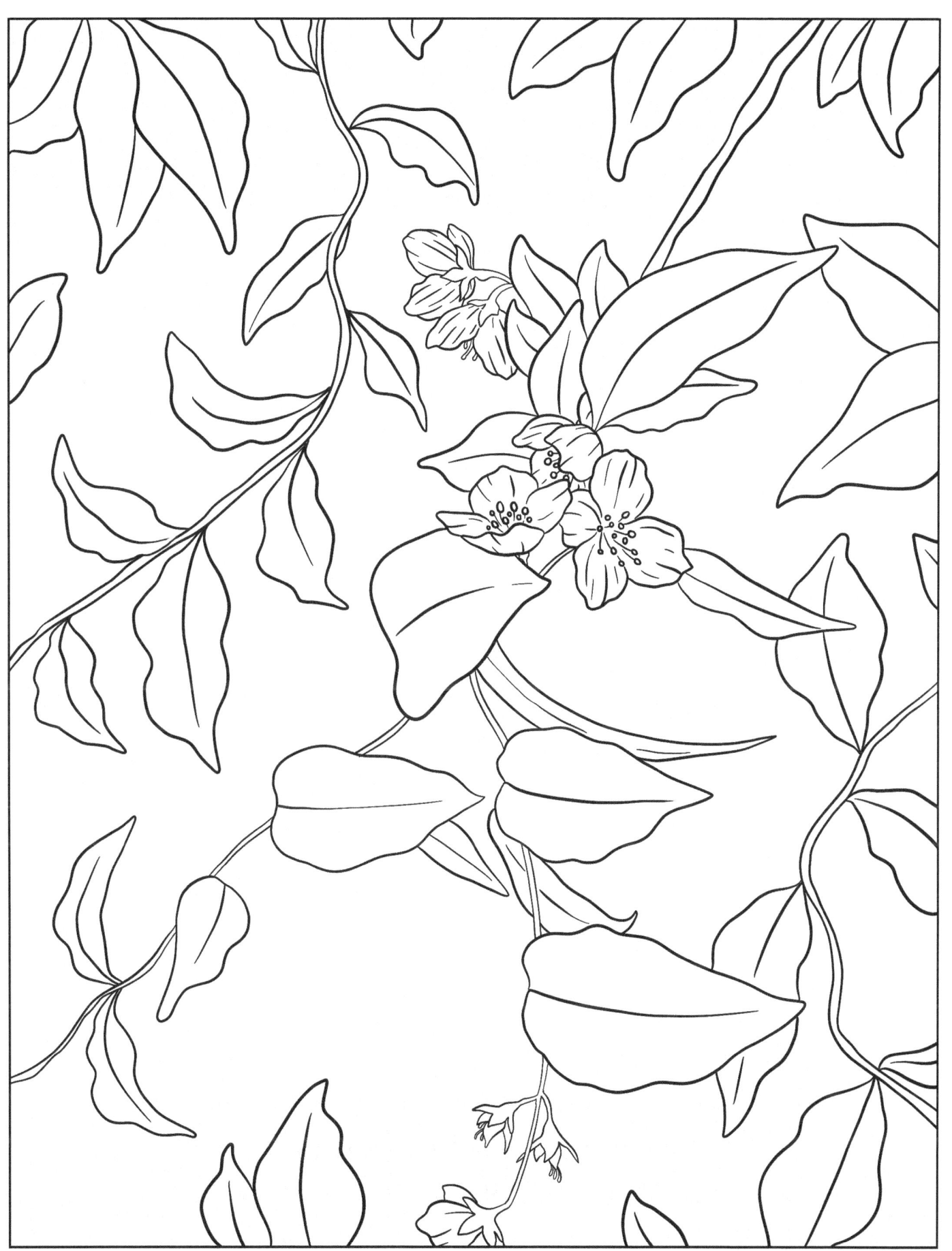

SCRIBBLE PAGE!

We've left this page blank, so you can test out your colors, cut out and frame your artwork, practice drawing flowers yourself, or tear it out and trace the designs onto watercolor paper, and have a go at painting them instead!

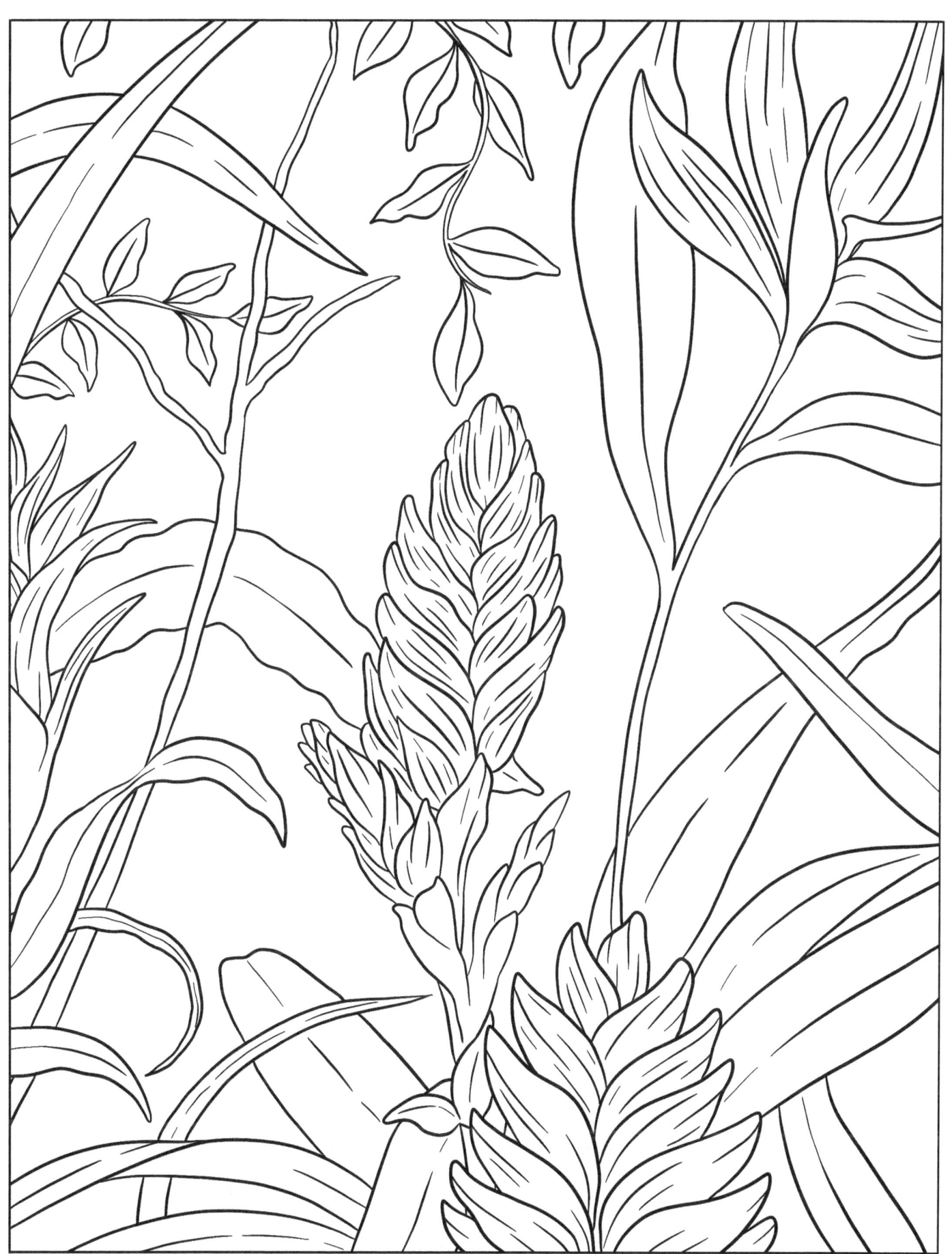

SCRIBBLE PAGE!

We've left this page blank, so you can test out your colors, cut out and frame your artwork, practice drawing flowers yourself, or tear it out and trace the designs onto watercolor paper, and have a go at painting them instead!

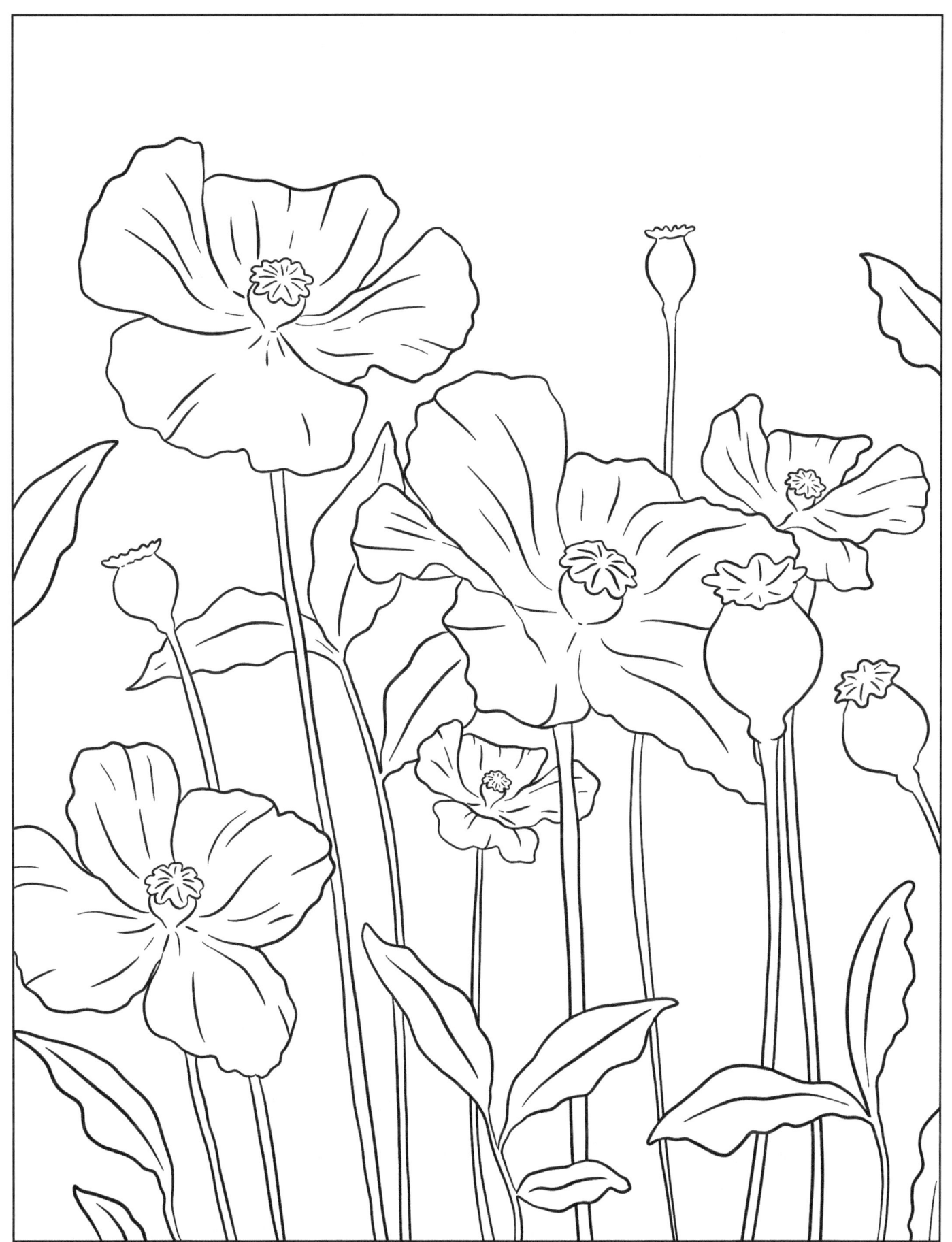

SCRIBBLE PAGE!

We've left this page blank, so you can test out your colors, cut out and frame your artwork, practice drawing flowers yourself, or tear it out and trace the designs onto watercolor paper, and have a go at painting them instead!

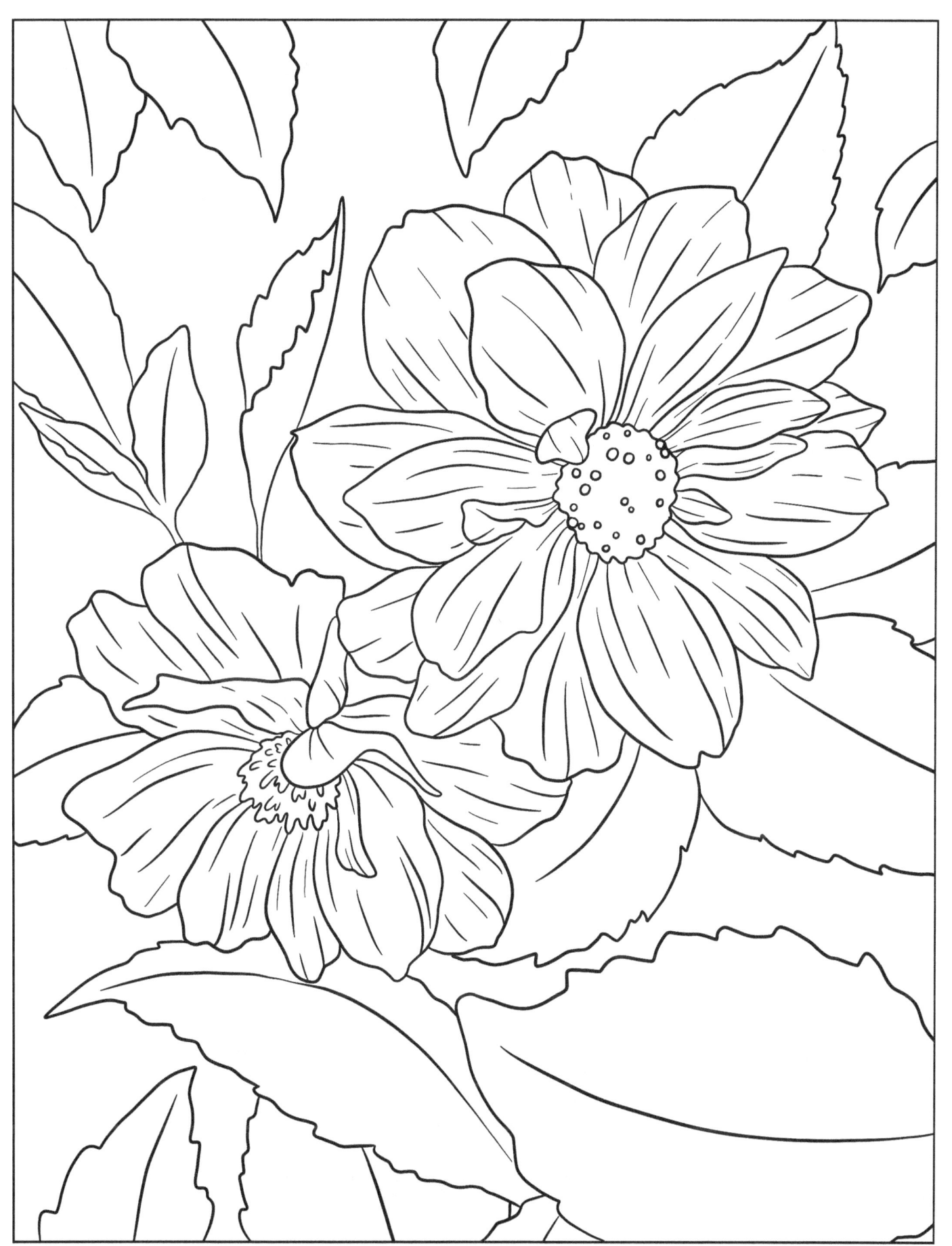

SCRIBBLE PAGE!
We've left this page blank, so you can test out your colors, cut out and frame your artwork, practice drawing flowers yourself, or tear it out and trace the designs onto watercolor paper, and have a go at painting them instead!

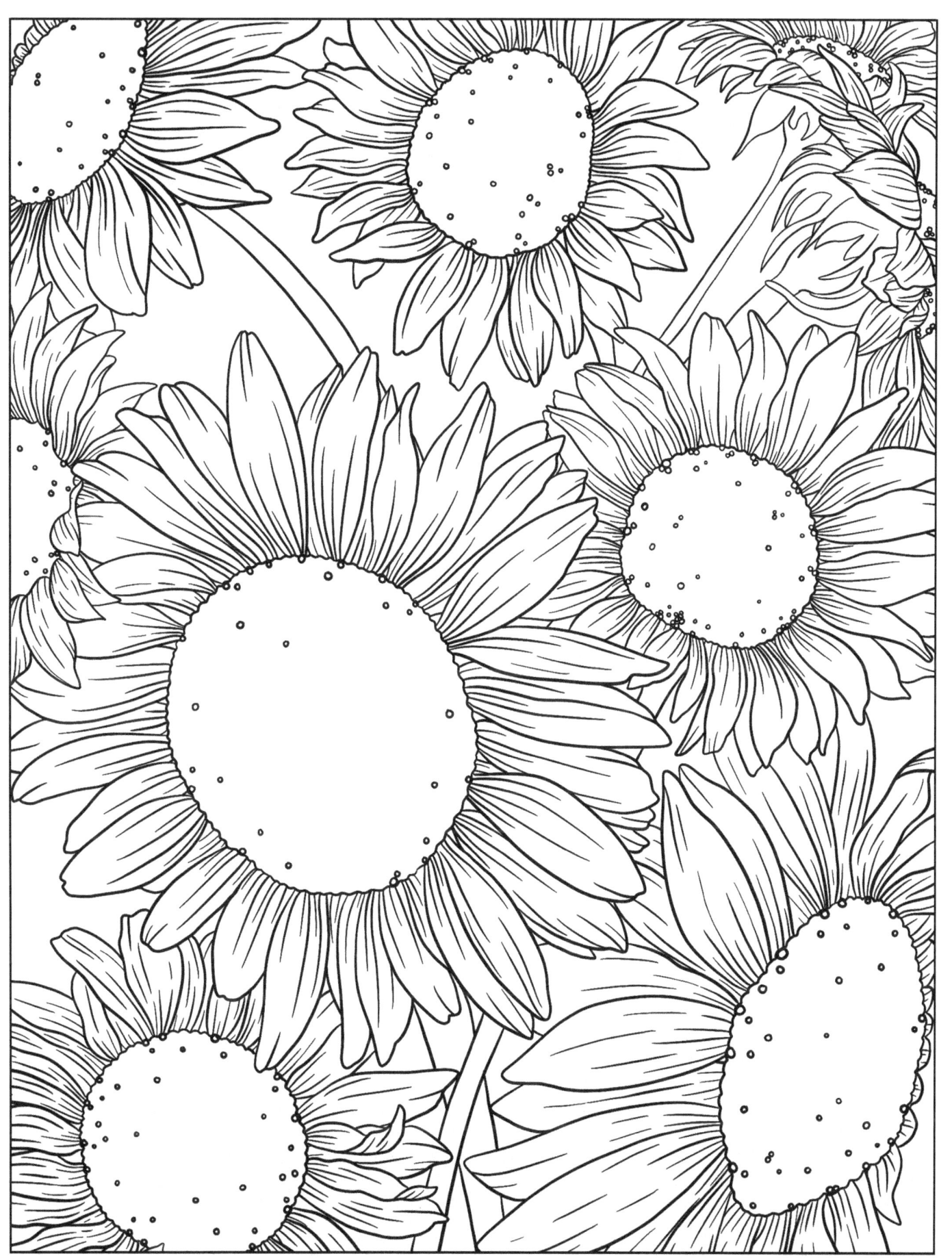

SCRIBBLE PAGE!

We've left this page blank, so you can test out your colors, cut out and frame your artwork, practice drawing flowers yourself, or tear it out and trace the designs onto watercolor paper, and have a go at painting them instead!

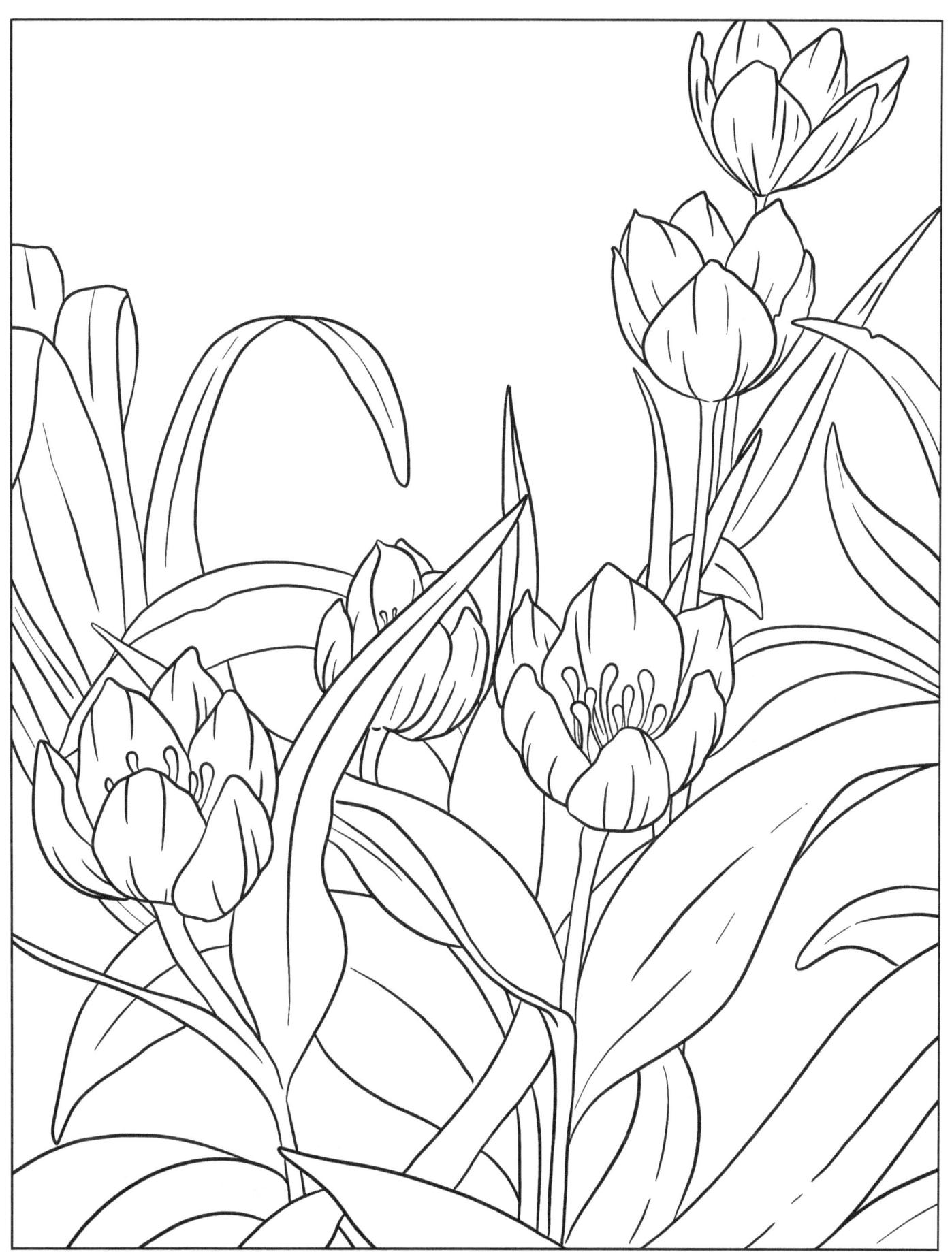

SCRIBBLE PAGE!

We've left this page blank, so you can test out your colors, cut out and frame your artwork, practice drawing flowers yourself, or tear it out and trace the designs onto watercolor paper, and have a go at painting them instead!

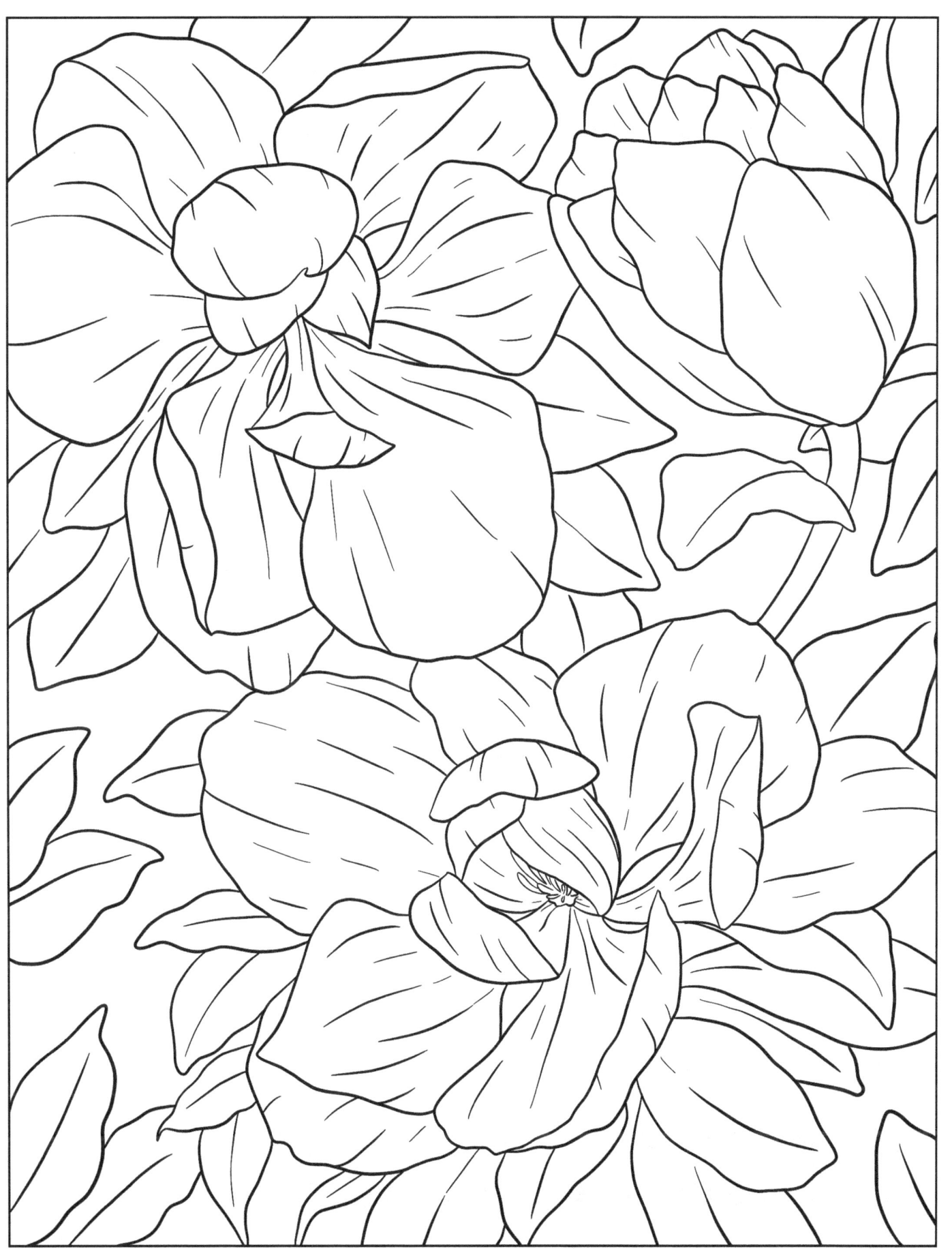

SCRIBBLE PAGE!

We've left this page blank, so you can test out your colors, cut out and frame your artwork, practice drawing flowers yourself, or tear it out and trace the designs onto watercolor paper, and have a go at painting them instead!

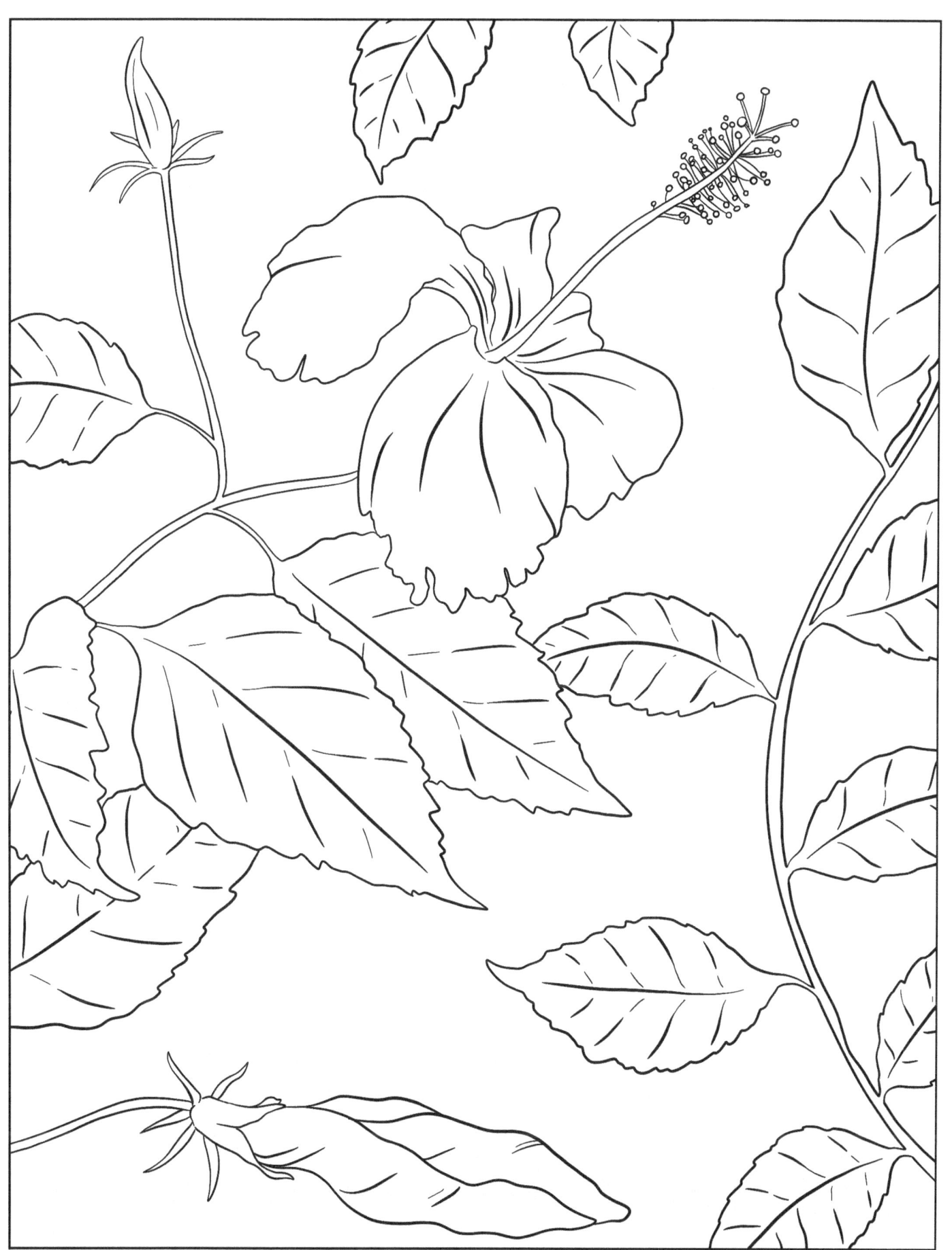

SCRIBBLE PAGE!

We've left this page blank, so you can test out your colors, cut out and frame your artwork, practice drawing flowers yourself, or tear it out and trace the designs onto watercolor paper, and have a go at painting them instead!

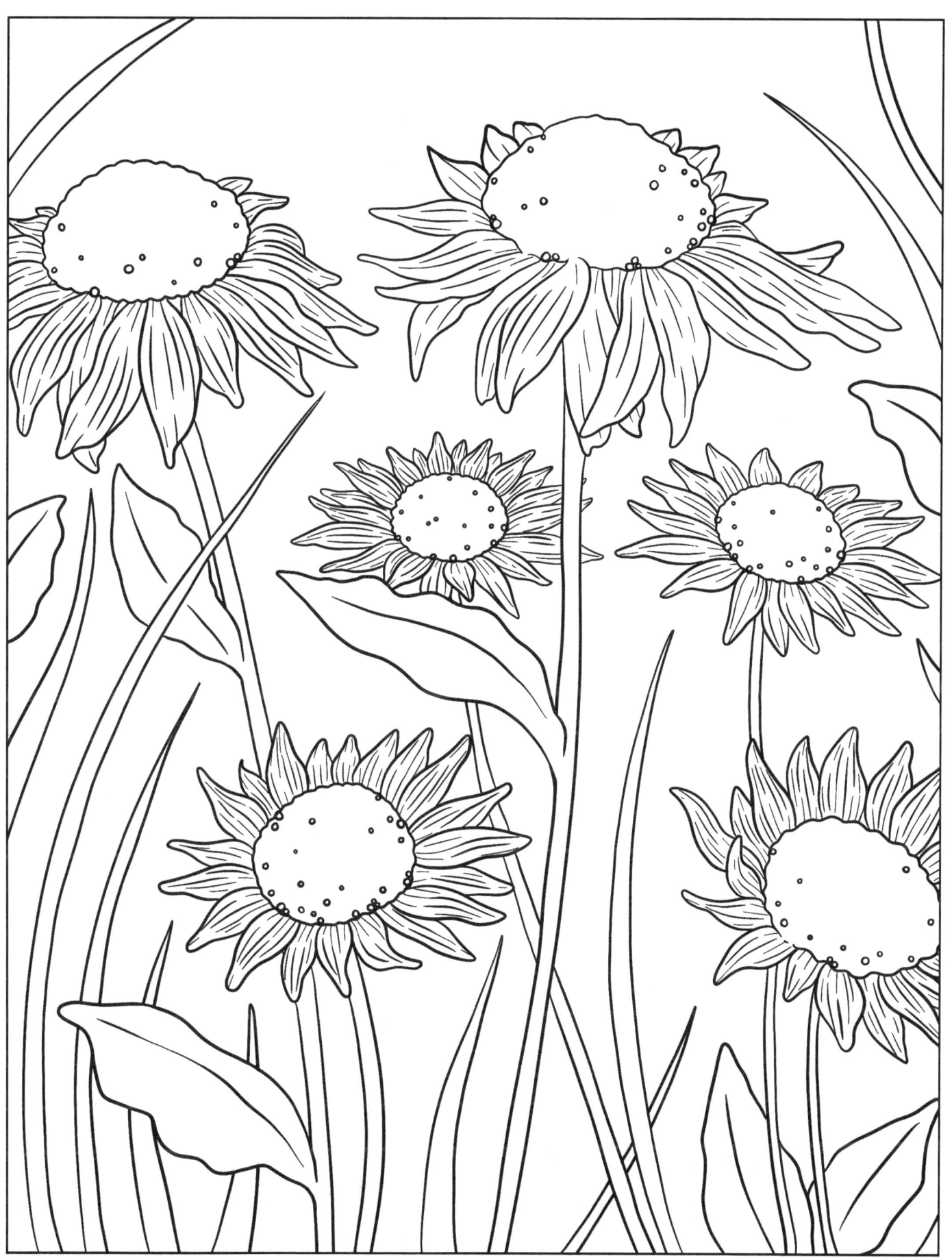

SCRIBBLE PAGE!

We've left this page blank, so you can test out your colors, cut out and frame your artwork, practice drawing flowers yourself, or tear it out and trace the designs onto watercolor paper, and have a go at painting them instead!

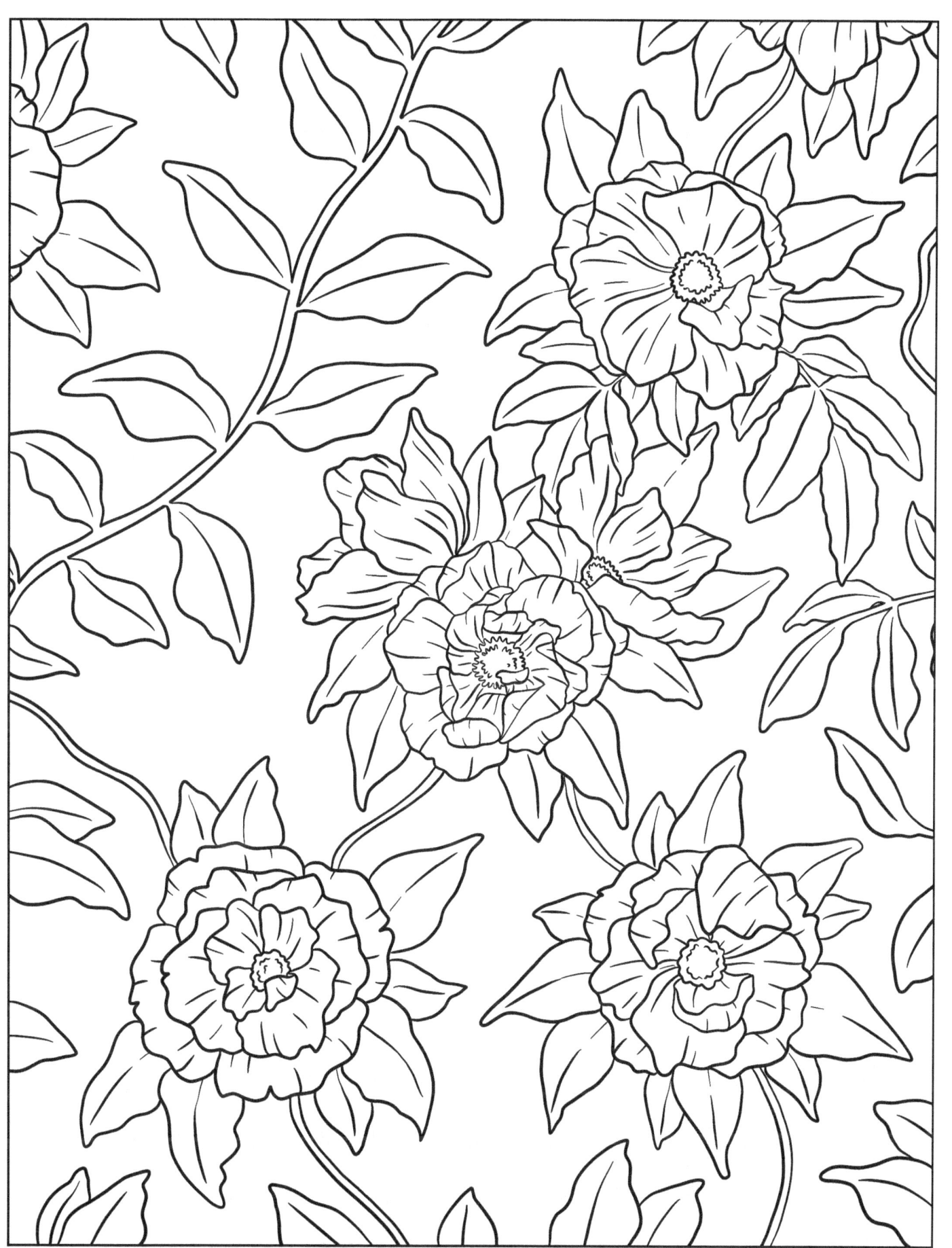

SCRIBBLE PAGE!

We've left this page blank, so you can test out your colors, cut out and frame your artwork, practice drawing flowers yourself, or tear it out and trace the designs onto watercolor paper, and have a go at painting them instead!

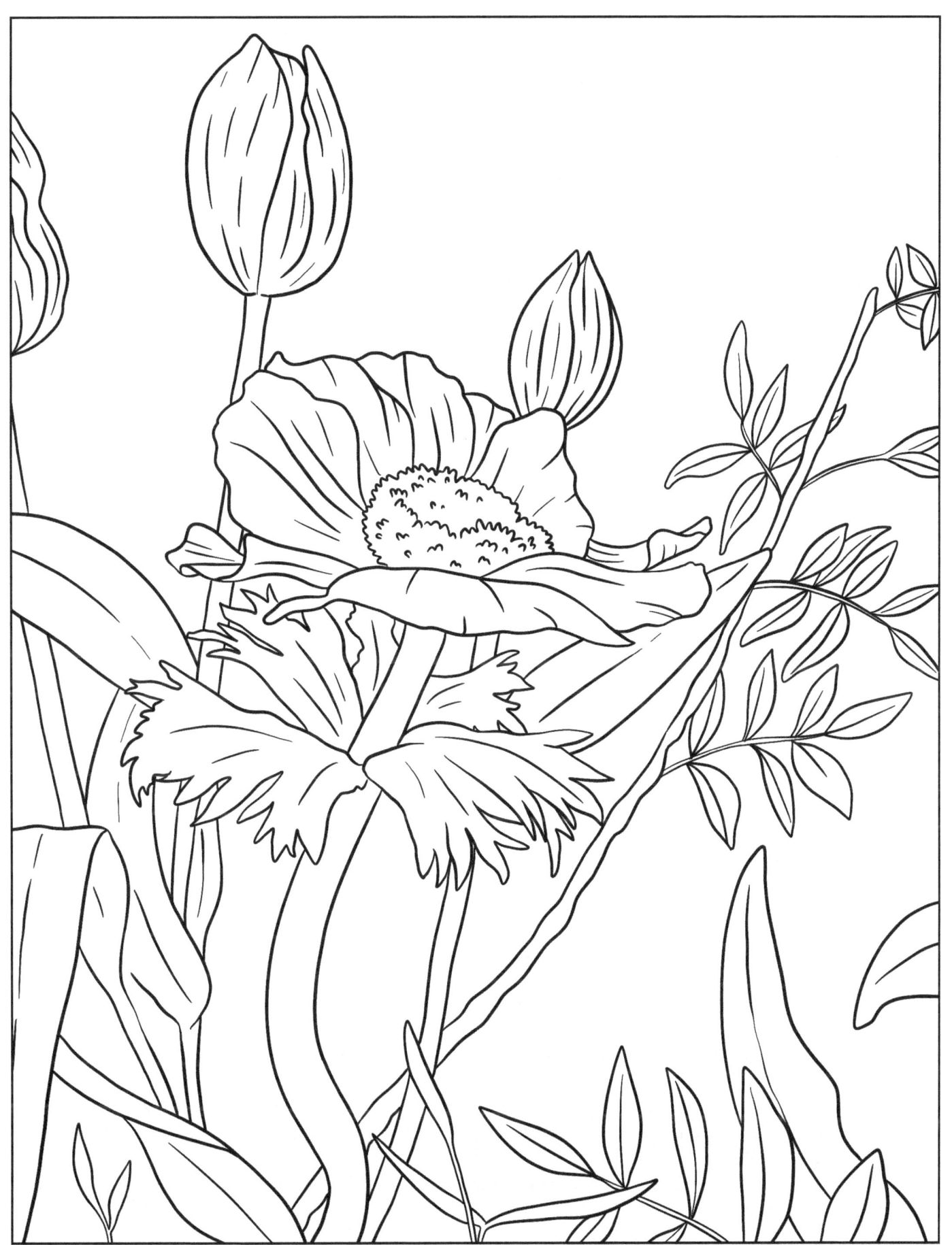

SCRIBBLE PAGE!
We've left this page blank, so you can test out your colors, cut out and frame your artwork, practice drawing flowers yourself, or tear it out and trace the designs onto watercolor paper, and have a go at painting them instead!

www.ingramcontent.com/pod-product-compliance
Lightning Source LLC
Chambersburg PA
CBHW080442220526
45465CB00007B/2736